Paul D. Bestolarides

THE FILM
PRODUCTION
HANDBOOK

1

PROLOGUE

Dear reader,

I have assembled a comprehensive handbook about the filmmaking process. The idea behind creating this manuscript occurred to me one day after recognizing that no books about film production exist. Inside, I present inquiries into the medium to augment learning for those who have taken an interest in this craft.

Beyond these pages are some personal and professional anecdotes about creating movies. In this rare instance, knowledge should be shared, rather than locked away.

TABLE OF CONTENTS

"Endurance is one of the most difficult disciplines, but it is the one that endures the final victory comes."

- Buddha

I.

INTRODUCTION TO MOTION PICTURES

The most interesting facet about movies is that motion pictures were discovered by accident. All of the entertainment houses that exist today from studios to cinema screens were not intended to exist. One of the inventors and acclaimed 'Father of Motion Pictures' was created by a photographer named Eadweard Muybridge who killed his Wife's lover and got away with murder by pleading insanity.

The medium of filmmaking has captivated the imagination of many. This manuscript is for those who want to learn the process of film production. The following text is an amalgamation of some experiences that I am comfortable with sharing.

Let's begin:

The visual medium of film operates as a *universal language* for mass communication. When people see a movie, they expect to see something visual. The visuals tell the story first. To prove this - look at silent films. They operated solely without dialogue to tell a story through emotion. Understanding the fundamental principle that visuals are a form of storytelling is paramount for progression.

In the medium of film, storytelling depends on visuals. Since cinema is a visual medium, it operates *pre-verbally,* which means the viewer understands the character's emotions on-screen before dialogue is exchanged. The entire medium is built upon human emotions for communication, before dialogue. The best evidence of this originates from the silent film era. The goal of a young filmmaker is to focus their awareness on telling a story through visuals and not rely too heavily on dialogue. See/read - Alexander MacKendricks *On Filmmaking.*

Here is an exercise - Think of your favorite moments in movies and your short film. The best moments are not dialogue scenes or character arcs. The best moments are the emotional reactions that captivated you as a viewer: how one actor reacts, the action sequence, or a revelation of a tragedy. Watch famous scenes from movies without sound. Ask yourself, can the story function without sound? You will be surprised that dialogue does not forward a scene, but the actions of characters do.

What does it take to pursue this industry?

This is one of the most frequently asked questions from students in my video courses. The answer is that anyone can pursue this industry, and it all depends on your mindset.

There is a poor way of thinking or a wealthy way of thinking.

The poor way of thinking is beating yourself up over what you don't have. 'I don't have money, connections, or talent.' That's the easiest way to lower your confidence. These are complaints; excuses for not trying. It's the complainers who expect something from the world, thinking the world should revolve around those who will not progress. These are the most miserable people because they blame others for their problems. It's easy to poison the mind, and find negativity in other people because it's a coping mechanism, but how far will this dissolution go to alter your perception of reality?

An aspiring filmmaker should answer the following:

- Identify: What do you want to study? How will you prepare for a filmmaking career? Is it a career, or just a hobby?

- Strengths & Weaknesses: Know your strengths and weaknesses. What genres do you enjoy? What are your weaknesses as a storyteller?

Many people are pursuing this industry with the mindset of 'trying to get in' as if there's some magical formula for status. So, they begin buying equipment, buying a lifestyle, and buying things outside of their means to prove themselves. In reality, they are buying a lifestyle they are unable to afford, to impress people they don't know, for a job that they have chosen not to research. It's the overconfident ones with expectations that have no chance of pursuing this industry.

On the other hand, there is a wealthy mindset. The wealthy mindset has nothing to do with finances, it's how you exercise your mind and engage with people. Only relationships can sustain you in this industry and acquiring knowledge of what you don't know will enable progression. Your mind is your greatest asset. Learning is always an opportunity whether you make mistakes, or accomplish a task. Your attempt at trying, by the motivation of your actions yields far greater results than never attempting anything. This is the risk-taking industry, you're going to make life changes and take risks, or you're going to regret not trying and remain in fear thinking money will enhance your lifestyle.

We live in a funny little world. A world so big that it's tiny. You hear yourself saying on occasion when meeting another, "What a small world." Indeed, it is. This is because if you apply yourself wholeheartedly to your interests by doing quality work, more industry contacts will come your way. Therefore, do not regret being in such a big industry because it gets smaller every time you progress. Instead of meeting people, you will meet better people. People that will help you grow, instead of others giving you their borrowed time.

You will find that you are not the only person sickened or frightened by human behavior. You are by no means alone when exterior events wrestle inside you. Many have been troubled emotionally, so much as spiritually. In this respect, someone will learn something from you, so much as you learn something from them. This human arrangement acts as a source of enlightenment in any stage of life. Therefore, it is important to follow your career ambitions to the end.

When I was a poor teenager wandering the streets with my 35mm film camera, I noticed that many people exchanged ideas, but the subject that was hotly debated among them was the subject of money. The most interesting part about listening in on their conversations was recognizing that most people in this world are not greedy, they are envious of others. Envy, being one of the deadly sins, corrupts the mind. I learned that wealth cannot be re-assured by bank accounts, it is by *appearance.*

Appearance can tell you a lot about somebody, even if it is just an appearance. Everyone wears a suit that not so much exists on the outside but is recognized from within. Some suits fit, others do not fit. After trial and error, you will get a better sense of the style that you choose to wear. Try on ideas, know your measurements, and dress your mind accordingly. Your mind is your greatest asset. My early years taught me that wealth in contemporary social classes of people [poor, middle-class, rich] was not based on financial income, but on how one thinks.

"There are three classes of people: those who see, those who do not see, and those who see when they are shown." - Leonardo DaVinci

A modern translation of this quote - People can see their ambitions flourish before they happen, others choose not to recognize their dreams, and then reality is to be perceived through revelation.

*

In 20th-century Britain, a man made a bet, claiming that he could escape from a jail cell under a specified time limit and free himself every time.

A new jail cell in the town was constructed with modern technology. The man accepted the challenge and was locked in the jail cell.

Hidden inside the man's belt was a 10 in. metal wire, a tool used for lock picking. As he began working the lock, he began to realize that his efforts were useless. Time passed and the man was drenched in sweat, realizing that he may be trapped. He collapsed in exhaustion, unable to escape. Then the jail cell door swung open, revealing that he had never been locked up in the first place.

In this moment, the man, famous escape artist Harry Houdini realized that 'It was my mind that kept me in prison.' Houdini, believed the cell door was locked based on his knowledge and his experience of escaping through other prison cells.

Houdini was known for his well-renowned escapes, but this escape served as a life lesson. He realized in that moment; that *my beliefs became my reality.*

There are many people in this world escaping life, who believe, like Houdini, that a door with a purpose of closing and locking is meant to remain that way. Although Houdini can escape from prison, many people suffer by staying within the prison of their minds. You can remain in a locked cell, struggling to escape, or see the door as a path to opportunity.

Houdini escaped life's physical threats, while we escape mental ones. Our minds have the power to see beyond ourselves or keep us from ourselves. As the famous philosopher Seneca stated - "We suffer more in imagination than in reality." Remember, you have power over your mind.

Take risks and learn.

THE INDUSTRY OF TODAY

Pre-Production - Ideas, Themes, and Storytelling.

Let's define filmmaking & videography -

Filmmaking - A story revealed through the visual medium intended for mass communication.

Videography - Creating content for a client to capture footage for a contractual means of publication.

Both terms are visual and require business knowledge. Their relationship extends through each phase of Production. I intend to provide insight on both mediums, respectfully.

Let's talk about the entertainment business

This is an industry that is constantly evolving, but here is one aspect of the industry that will never change - There are many areas in this industry that you can explore and you may be surprised that some of your favorite creators dabble in many areas. Whether you want to produce videos or make movies, realize: *how you see yourself is how people see you.* You are not only going to make films; you are going to be the next innovation. Only you know your worth.

A lawyer from Warner Bros. once told me "Movies and videos don't sell themselves. The value of your name does."

You see it all the time from promotional advertisements to movie trailers and the names of the creators. You know their name and their work, more than the project that they are currently selling. This industry knows that audiences buy names, not necessarily the quality of the story.

Now that you understand this element of the industry, you have to find a way to sustain the business by 'showing' content.

This is a 'show don't tell industry.' Talking only gets you so far, but if you're not showing what you're made of, nobody will invest in you. This is one of the largest problems with the industry today - Too many fake content creators -You see tons of advertisers, gurus, and YouTubers trying to sell you content to provide their experience, but they have nothing to show. Why? Because they are too busy making videos for YouTube instead of making movies.

Here are the reasons to <u>not</u> pursue this industry – If you're doing it for the money if you think talking your way in to persuade people will benefit your career, and if you are in it for the short term.

Now that you know something about the entertainment business, realize that it is a business that you have to create for yourself. There are ways of obtaining a career, but with great effort comes great sacrifice. Most are freelancers in this industry. That's a difficult lifestyle, but it's an income and can be closer to one's interests. This is an industry of dreams, dreams fulfilled, and dreams crushed. Above all, this is your industry, and only you can change it.

Allow me to provide a real-life example of a student who changed her life based on this mindset. It was my second semester of teaching at San Joaquin Delta College and this student completed my advanced course but never returned to the department until months later.

Below is a transcription of our conversation:

"I am interested in working on-set," the student said.

I smiled and replied: "I have an upcoming short film and will give you the PA position, and you will volunteer for free."

"What if I don't perform well on set?" she asked.

I looked her straight in the eye and replied, "I just gave you an opportunity, take it or leave it."

She took the opportunity. This student had a full-time job outside of school - stacking boxes at an Amazon warehouse.

She worked on-set for 3 days. After the experience, we chatted on the phone. She enjoyed being on-set and my friends thought she performed well. One of my friends, an Assistant Director, was working as a Production Assistant professionally, and considered her for more jobs.

During the phone call with the student, she thanked me for the experience with a newfound interest in Production.

I began the conversation: "Now that we have wrapped up Production, I will tell you that I paid everyone else on-set except you. You worked for free to see if you liked the experience. So, did you enjoy the experience?"

"Yes, I learned so much more than in the classroom."

I laughed. "Yes, you made friends with like-minded interests and learned what it's like to be on-set. Even though you worked for free, which job do you prefer, working on-set or getting paid to stack boxes at Amazon?"

"Working on-set for sure. I didn't care about working for free, I was learning."

"Right. Now you understand the value of time. When you work hard for what you don't want, you are not learning anything new and are only working for the reward, but when you work at what you do want, you provide time by learning and the reward feels better. Now that my Assistant Director friend has seen your work on set, you don't have to apply for jobs. Watch her give them to you. You will realize that even though you worked for free, you have generated value in yourself making more people interested in working with you. Now that you are worth more by the value that you produced, you can make more money at a job you enjoy."

The student went on to work on tv shows, and major studios like Disney and others. Her name is seen in the credits to this day on streaming services and she continues working on-set, now for the local news.

Take risks, and learn. There is no room to complain or beat yourself up over what you don't know. You have just as much opportunity as anyone else to obtain advice, research, and focus on your goals. You are perfectly capable of achieving goals, and are closer to obtaining success with your business, turning your dreams into reality. Do not discard an experience based on personal finances.

As Warren Buffet famously said, "The best investment you can ever make is in yourself." Only you can progress. Once you invest in yourself, you will realize the importance of time.

One of the major problems in our society is that people will take any job they don't like for money, instead of investing in what interests them. One's finances can be perceived as oxygen because it is necessary for survival, but it should not be treated as life-support [taking you away from your ambitions]. In my experience, when you lose everything, *valuing* what you still have is a reminder to bounce back stronger. Life is absurd in the sense that dependency on finances can enhance or cripple one's career pursuits.

The Greek figure Sisyphus was condemned by the gods for eternity to repeatedly roll a boulder up a hill only to have it roll down again once he got it to the top is a metaphor for the individual's persistent struggle against life's absurdities. Everyone shares the same fate - they must work to satisfy a lifestyle. Some people would rather sacrifice their minds for what they don't want, instead of putting their minds to work by focusing on what they do want.

So, let's assume that for the remainder of this manuscript, we are taking the approach to a wealthy mindset.

*

Now we are ready to discuss the Production phases [The 3 P's]. The three production phases The phases identify the status of the project.

Let's begin by discussing ideas.

II.

PRE-PRODUCTION

Where do ideas come from?

Answer: Dreams, life experiences, books, relationships, memories, etc. There are ideas everywhere so long as you notice. *[See The Kybalion, pg. 136].*

Every story is rooted in myth. According to the ancient Greek philosopher Plato, 'Art imitates nature.'

Theme - The primary focus subject explored in a piece of writing.

Pre-Production - The preparatory stages before Production.

On the subject of Mythology

Myths help us navigate our lives by revealing a fundamental aspect of human life. They are stories of wisdom. The characters are usually gods or supernatural beings. Mythology tells us how we relate to the natural world, from one's community to the cosmos, underpinning all life and harmonizing with the universe, or informing us when these elements conflict. Myths exist to show us the omens of the universe. A myth takes one on a spiritual journey of enlightenment, expressed in symbolic form.

A god is a motivating power that functions in human life and the universe. Creation and destruction are a function of the universe. This being is personified in ourselves. Those powers flow through us too. The same power that emanates from you, emanates the whole universe.

A professor and Anthropologist of comparable mythology named Joseph Campbell wrote a book titled, *The Hero with a Thousand Faces* (1949).

Joseph Campbell's 4 functions of myth:

Mystical – Revealing the mystery underlying all things and being. 2. Cosmological – Relating to the universe and the way the world works.

Sociological – They support and order the society that created the myth.

Pedagogical – A teaching mechanism to guide us, enabling us to situate ourselves in that story that awakens us.

Campbell coins the term 'monomyth,' relating to the significance that all stories share a singular journey called 'The Hero's Journey.'

'The Hero's Journey' is the common template of stories that involve a hero who is transformed after their experience.

In Act I, the main character (protagonist), is a lesser version of a hero. The protagonist desires change in their life from their ordinary world, but they refuse the call to adventure. They meet a mentor; a guide that re-invigorates passion into the protagonist to follow their calling.

The protagonist then enters the special (extraordinary) world in Act II and meets allies and enemies. At the Midpoint, they accomplish the first goal but lose someone close to them.

They encounter an 'All is Lost' moment, and are then inspired to accomplish their final goal.

In Act III the final goal is accomplished, they return to the ordinary world and take not only their newly founded knowledge but also the discovery of the self.

During a broadcast interview, Joseph Campbell stated:

"Heroes are worth writing about. A hero is someone who has given his life to something bigger than himself. There is a physical deed containing the external journey containing heroism, sacrificing himself to another. The spiritual hero has found a mode of experiencing a supernormal way of spiritual life and has come back to communicate it. The main character is someone who has found or achieved something beyond the normal range of experience. There is a going and a return and this is what the hero cycle represents.

This journey can also be conveyed in an initiation ritual, or a 'rite of passage' where a child has to give up their childhood, to become a self-responsible adult.

The hero's journey is a fundamental experience that everyone has to undergo. All of us must escape a psychological dependency and responsibility requires death and resurrection which is the motif of the hero's journey. Leaving one condition, finding the source of life to bring you into understanding for a richer life experience."

These old stories live in us. The stages of human development are the same today as they were in ancient times.

All myths evoke a self-authority (maturity) transformation.

Analysis of Myth & and its Structure

Myth is often associated with fiction, but there is always truth to fiction. A universal truth of being, revealing mystical parts of the universe to us.

Screenwriting & Visual Literacy

Screenwriting – Themes

Let's talk about the modern industry of screenwriters.

Many filmmakers have voiced their opinions on social media about the changing ways of the industry. What they have in common is their revelation about their experience - if you are trying to become a screenwriter, *don't expect a career in selling your scripts.*

A true writer writes for themselves without the external distractions of material needs, fame, and companionship.

Now that you know something about the entertainment business, realize that it is a business that you have to create for yourself. There are ways of obtaining a career, but with great effort comes great sacrifice. Most are freelancers in this industry. That's a difficult lifestyle, but it's an income closer to one's interests. This is an industry of dreams, dreams fulfilled, and dreams crushed. There are no two ways about it, but it's the knowledge and experience, learning what you don't know that is, for some, worth knowing. It's your industry, and only you can change it.

I have seen people trying to sell scripts, but in reality, the industry has so much content, that studios are not interested in buying or soliciting scripts. There are professional writers in the industry who can be hired for that.

The idea of selling a script is based on the old industry of the '80s and '90s where screenplays were in demand for new writers who would pay a significant amount for an option deal, or sell.

Today's industry has changed. The industry of the past invested in people, the industry of today embraces technology.

To further my case, look at all of the original scripts made for movies. How many original scripts do you see made per year? That's right, not very many. Pre-pandemic, and even now it's the industry of remakes and sequels. Recycling old ideas for a massive payout. Fan service and nostalgic throwbacks to get people back in the theatre.

The competition, streaming services. How many original scripts are made? A lot more, but there's a similarity with studio films. Have you noticed? The name of the writing credit is the same as the directing credit. Only well-established directors can write their content. Why? Because they know the script, they know the business and they are the only ones qualified to move projects forward.

There is no interest in new screenwriters, whether you have a good story or not, doesn't matter. These executives want to know if you can direct them too. Case in point, I pitched to 3 studios at a prestigious film festival. The writers exiting that meeting room said they were surprised they weren't chosen for their writing efforts. And that's when I leveraged my abilities. I knew from the beginning that no one would care about my stories unless I realized them. That's why I also play the role of director. Once I mentioned this at the pitch meeting, their ears perked up.

Your writing only goes so far. If you are trying to be a writer in this industry, you're going to begin in television as there is far more content there. Television writers have changed. Now several groups of people are involved with the writing process. Writers are shuffled around all the time.

If you want to be a screenwriter for movies, then you are going to become a director or find a friend to direct your story. That is your only chance of selling in this industry today unless you move to the industry and work in television. I do not see this format changing post-covid as there is more of an abundance of content. They have been working this way for 30-something years. There's a reason why it works. Prove yourself first and obtain the opportunity to write through directing. It's tough, but not impossible.

For all of you wanting to be screenwriters, here is my advice – learn directing, find a friend who will direct your movie, or write novels. I realized in my early years of screenwriting selling your script is like giving your baby away. You have no idea what the buyers like, so you might as well do it right yourself.

As Steven Spielberg emphasizes, "If it's not on the page, it's not on the stage." If you're not writing, it won't be realized on screen.

In Pre-production, we defined the theme and its relation to storytelling. Next, we studied visual literacy – how to make sense of the image. While looking at movies, the visuals informed the viewer of the story. People watch videos to see something visual first. Lastly, we discussed the role of the screenwriter and how writing develops a story.

DEVELOPING CHARACTERS

Let us jump into storytelling. I will further discuss ideas by showcasing the importance of screenwriting theory and formatting.

Not all of us want to be screenwriters, but I believe knowing the format is important for any position on-set, screenwriter or not. We will begin with screenwriting theory, and then transition into learning the format.

The Logline - A condensed version of what your story is about. This idea exists because, as you may know, ideas fuel the industry, but not everyone has the time and energy to hear a long-winded description of the story.

Loglines exist all around us. You can find a 1-2 sentence description of the story while scrolling through the streaming services, searching for them on IMDb, or applications. They exist for a reason – to summarize your idea for maximum impact.

There are no rules about writing the Logline, but I have discovered the most effective ones rely on four principles – Protagonist, Antagonist, Central Problem, and Setting.

For those of you not aware of these terms, allow me to explain.

-The Protagonist - The central focus of the story and has a recognizable goal. As the audience or reader, the protagonist obtains the most experience throughout the story.

Oftentimes, people misinterpret the protagonist as the hero who has to change. This can be the attributes of the protagonist, but it is not concrete. I think people often misjudge the real definition because they are used to seeing superhero films and movies where the protagonist changes and fights the bad guy, which leads me to the next description.

-The Antagonist - Opposes the goals of the protagonist. They do not have to be a villain or evil, but they can. The Antagonist opposes the views and goals of the Protagonist.

The most effective stories originate from characters who have CLEAR similarities and differences. Let's use an example.

Let's use the DC comic book story of Batman and the Joker. Let's start with their similarities.

Batman and Joker experienced one bad day that changed their life forever. Batman's parents died, and the Joker became hideously disfigured.

Batman [AKA Bruce Wayne] falls into the Bat-cave, which mentally changes his outlook on life.

The Joker falls in acid, which physically changes his outlook on life as a result of his appearance.

Both characters leverage fear to their advantage. Batman hides behind a mask, scaring criminals. The Joker shows his true self and always wears his face paint and, in some iterations, Joker wants Batman to reveal his true self by removing his mask for all to see.

Both characters want to change Gotham City. Batman believes that eliminating crime can create a better world. Joker believes that there is a lot of corruption hidden from the public eye and revealing the corruption, can create a better world.

Let's identify the differences:

Batman fights for vengeance. The Joker, for anarchy. In some iterations, both characters take pleasure in beating others up, which haunts them mentally.

Batman is rich, and the Joker is poor. Both characters co-exist on opposite ends of society.

For Batman, Joker presents mental challenges.

For Joker, Batman presents a physical challenge.

What about side characters? The same idea is emphasized:

The detective Jim Gordon is friends with Batman. As a police Lieutenant, he also fights crime but doesn't hide behind a mask. Batman and Gordon believe in peace for Gotham and they dislike criminals like the Joker. Joker also manipulates Gordon to get closer to Batman.

All of the characters complement each other and provide contrasting viewpoints so that the audience can realize their motivations.

Now that you understand the definition of protagonist, antagonist, and central characters, let's discuss the setting. The setting is the primary location where the action takes place.

~In a galaxy far far away, in a shopping mall, or on a train. The setting is driving the premise situating characters in an environment where they are forced to make choices.

Let's think about stories for a moment. We have all collectively heard of storytelling terms. Plot, Character, Tragedy. But where do these terms come from, and how do we make sense of them?

According to anthropologist Joseph Campbell, storytelling comes from mythology, from our ancestors of the past, but the Ancient Greeks innovated storytelling through theatre and established the definitions for the elements of story.

The Classical philosopher, Aristotle wrote the Poetics, a manuscript defining stories and how to make sense of them. Most notably, the film industry and screenwriters continue to use Aristotle as a reference for storytelling today. Aristotle clearly defines storytelling and how each of the elements plays in harmony with one another. We know that the Ancient Greeks created plays, not movies, but the ideas still resonate even to this day.

Aristotle defines

Plot, character, spectacle, Thought, Song, Diction. Aristotle claims that these elements make up the story. Let's identify each of them.

- Plot - A series of events.

- Character The subject(s) of focus

- Spectacle - The visual components

- Thought - The overall intention of the writing

- Diction - The language spoken by characters

- Song - The lyricism from the dialogue.

Within the elements of the story, exists 3 foundations for the Plot:

Peripeteia (Perip-et-ayea) – Reversal of Fortune

Anagnorisis (Anag-nor-isis) – Recognition, or discovery of truth

40

Suffering – Destructive or painful action.

Let's define Tragedy-

Tragedy makes up all genres in some way shape or form – Tragedy is defined as an imitation of an action that is serious, complete, and of a certain magnitude.

What does Aristotle mean by imitation you ask? Aristotle believes that art reflects life and that everything created is merely an imitation of nature transformed through storytelling elements.

Now that we know something about Aristotle, Let's apply Aristotle's theories to another story. For this example, we will use:

The Lion King

Simba is the protagonist. Scar is the Antagonist. We know this because – we are seeing the kingdom through Simba's perspective and identifying with his primary goal.

Both characters want to be King

Simba is changed mentally, Scar, is changed physically.

Scar changes the course of events by eliminating the previous King, Simba's father.

Simba becomes transformed by the tragedy of the death of his father, which is humanly relatable or serves as an imitation of nature. Everyone has experienced the death of a loved one and learned how to cope with it by transforming their lives. This is why audiences believe in Simba's cause.

Simba has to suffer throughout the film to realize that he is the best fit for King.

What makes the story of The Lion King exciting is that the audience knows Scar killed Simba's father, but Simba does not know [dramatic irony]. So, the audience is waiting for the reveal. Scar reveals this information to Simba later, which, is the Anagnorisis (Anag-nor-isis). In the end, there is Peripeteia (Perip-et-area), or a reversal of fortune, Simba becomes King, and Scar perishes.

*

All good stories require structure. This is a discipline that will enhance your writing abilities. All stories are *'Who does what, with which, to whom, and why?'*

I have not read many screenwriting books over the years, but I do find a few to be helpful. Aristotle's Poetics is one example. The reason why I do not read too many books about filmmaking is that most of the writers are theorists and are not a part of the film industry. They are just as bad as the YouTubers trying to sell you an experience, or wanting you to join their seminars, claiming they're gurus. Overall, I trust writers who have experience. Before buying a book about filmmaking or videography, be sure to do your research.

EXPOSITION

<u>Exposition</u> - When a character(s) explain or exchange information about a significant plot detail.

Exposition is the writer's way of giving background information to the audience about the characters and/or setting of the story.

Exposition is the most difficult form of writing because it does not operate through visuals and breaks the 'show don't tell' ideology.

Bad writing is noticeable when the writer disregards the intelligence of the characters and the viewer.

Here are a few tips for writing compelling expositional moments:

1. Use [tension/conflict] between characters to enhance their interaction. [Ex: In *The Prestige*, Nolan utilizes fast edits to describe a character's feelings toward another].

2. Use an object of interest [visual prop(s)] to visually persuade the viewer of an idea. [Ex: In DePalma's *Mission Impossible*, Tom Cruise uses a magic trick to discuss the importance of their mission, but to also foil another character's plan. The dialogue scene is long but Cruises' sleight of hand techniques keep us entertained].

3. Use setting to compliment the dialogue through visuals. [Ex: In Kubrick's *The Shining*, Jack and Grady have a conversation about the living and the dead in a restroom covered in monochromatic red [foreshadowing murder]. In this presentation the viewer sees the conversation unfold visually through the set design.

4. Input plausibility into the conversation where a character's response is set up by their knowledge about the subject.

Example of a bad exposition - A sibling describing to their younger brother about their life situation. If the siblings grew up together, why would they speak to each other in this way? Instead of the writer situating themselves like the characters, they pivot to the exchange of implausible dialogue.

Example of a good exposition - In Spielberg's *Indiana Jones and the Last Crusade*, a wealthy patron describes the backstory of the Holy Grail to Indian Jones in the setting of a <u>visually</u> pleasing office. The four-minute conversation includes complex blocking where the exchange of dialogue happens by introducing three <u>visual props</u>: The sacred tablet, a wine glass, and an ancient text manuscript. Although passing the wine glass to Jones is a nice gesture, Jones later becomes skeptical of the man's pursuit of the grail, creating <u>tension.</u> Once the wealthy patron passes Jones the wine glass he tells him, "…The Holy Grail Dr. Jones. The chalice used by Christ during the Last Supper. The cup that caught his blood at the crucifixion and was entrusted to Joseph of Arimathea."

Indiana Jones interjects and says, "The Arthur legend. I've heard this bedtime story before…"

Since the audience is already aware that Indiana Jones is a University professor who excels in the subject of anthropology, the plausibility of a professor knowing a historical story is believable.

As the conversation continues, the wealthy patron invites Indiana Jones over to view a visual prop of an ancient text manuscript of the friar chronicling the knights' story.

This is a good example of exposition because the scene is presented in a plausible dialogue exchange that is visually pleasing to the viewer. The presentation of the dialogue scene satisfies the viewer's interest by 'showing and telling.'

To summarize this lecture – Ideas should be formulated within the logline to provide clarity to others. Once the Logline is polished, it is time to physically write the script. The philosopher, Aristotle is a guide to knowing the contents of a story. A writer must then grow their skill set in the craft and be interesting. The most uninteresting form of writing is exposition, but the provided expositional tips will assist you in becoming a better storyteller. Next, we looked at industry formatting. Even if you are not interested in becoming a screenwriter, you should understand screenplay formatting in other positions.

APPROACHING SCREENWRITING

Remember: A script is written to be read fast. Remove poetic flowery language. As author Raymond Carver famously said - "With storytelling; get in and get out."

Now that we understand something about writing theory, let's jump into formatting.

Screenplays have kept the same format since the beginning. It's one element in the industry that has not changed.

The font of choice for screenplay formatting is - `Courier`.

The industry uses this font because it is not only easy to read, it is a typewritten font that was originally written on typewriters.

Keeping everything in the present tense tells the reader what is happening in real time as if watching the actions play out on screen.

ALL CAPS are used for elements of importance, character introductions, sounds, and transitions.

Only describe what is necessary for the scene. Screenplays are not like novels, with long-winded descriptions or poetic flair. Screenplays are written because they are meant to be read fast. Less description invites collaboration for other departments on set to be a part of the creative process.

Writing at a 5th-grade level isn't a rule, but it is a guideline. Keep it simple, not complex.

Now that you know something about screenplay formatting, we move on to bringing the vision to life.

SHOT LISTING/STORYBOARDS

Now that you have written your story, you will have to convey your vision to others. You have the cast and crew hired, but there is still more to plan. This is where shot listing and storyboarding come into play.

A shot list is a detailed outline of what you plan to shoot. It keeps the filmmakers in line and on schedule to execute the shot as intended. Storyboards help identify these ideas visually. There are no rules of having to complete both or one over the other. That is entirely reliant on you, however, the more you plan, the better the results. I draw out every single shot in my films. This way, I am closer to bringing my vision to life with accuracy. It also helps others realize my vision and proves my organizational skills.

Although my method takes more time, I think it is worth the effort.

*

After a screening of my first festival-ready short film, a man close to my age wanted to hire me to work on a reality TV show for a couple of months. I humbly accepted the offer and we became friends. I was 3 years into film directing at the time (24 years old), and he was 3 years into working on sets. He enjoyed speaking with me because he desired to be a writer/director like myself. I wanted more experience on set, so our friendship was complimentary.

Almost a year later, we met up for lunch. He graciously paid for my meal. He looked at me and smiled while I ate my sandwich.

-Paul, when are you going to get out of teaching and move to L.A. and work in the film industry?

-I replied, 'Teaching part-time pushes me closer toward studio directing. I plan to move to L.A. after the completion of my first feature-length film. Teaching allows me to sustain creative flexibility that works twofold. When I make a film and bring students on set, they can obtain a career. Teaching also allows me to practice/use equipment in both an educational and professional setting.

-But teaching filmmaking is not like being on-set, and pushes you further away from experience. I am sacrificing my time, taking great gigs, sleeping in my car, meeting people, and working on sets. I have worked on many sets and know producers.

-That depends on your perception.

-What do you mean?

-Since the beginning of our friendship, you've wanted to write and direct. So do I, except I am actually doing it. You accuse me of lacking experience, yet you are playing the role of a Production Assistant for Reality TV shows, not a film director.

-But I put in hard work. People see me on-set. They don't see you in a classroom.

-Now you have highlighted the difference between how we think. You have been *working hard* in this industry at what you don't want - being a Production Assistant in Television, yet you stress Directing Films. I *work smart* at what I do want, which is Directing and that's how people see me. After all, the reason we met was because you took an interest in me. After all, I am a director. Therefore, your argument is insufficient. Do people see you as a Director, or do you express your interest in Directing on-set to others?

-But at least I'm on set!

-Yes, but knowing a Producer as a Director is far different than a Production Assistant. Who would they trust more, a director who shows work and has won awards, or a Production Assistant who dreams about it?

-You don't know the business like I do, you have never sold your films. In 2 years of being a Production Assistant, I have made a lot of money, more than your teaching job.

-Correct, because you work more hours than me, and once again, you work hard *at what you don't want.*

-If you knew this industry well, you would be selling, but you're too busy throwing away money to create personal projects. I wrote a draft based on your short film that is far superior to your original idea. We can get investors to fund it. We just need $15,000.

-In my opinion, that is far too much for a short film. I don't think investors are a good idea for short form.

-That's why you don't get it. You're too afraid of risk. Maybe that's why you are unable to sell your films and remain in a classroom.

- *I foolishly was angered at his last comment, and my reply deepened the wound:* I will sell this film without your advice. Since you know producing and directing so well, you can make your own films. You don't need me around for help. I'm not afraid of risk, because I make movies, but something keeps you from making them and it appears to be money. What a waste of a life to think that money will fuel your creativity and like a fool, you think money will make you a successful director.

We left that day bitter with one other.

This old friend spent his college years partying and waiting tables at restaurants. It was true, that he put in hard work, but there was a catch, it was about the desire to be seen and looking for money. Did he make the same mistake again, now as a Production Assistant? I think so.

At the end of that year, I followed through with my ambitions and ended up selling all of my short films which continue to have worldwide distribution to this day. Also to this day, the old friend continues to work as a Production Assistant/Editor for Reality TV in L.A. I prefer being a continuing Writer/Director myself.

Perception and how we interpret it defines us. The Roman philosopher Marcus Aurelius once wrote: *Harness objectivity and see the world through a new vantage point. Continue moving further away outside your perspective, to learn about the world.* A few days after speaking with this person, I regretted my comments because my insults came from anger, but after taking a step back, I realized that the past was unalterable. I was young and in my vulnerable years, but what mattered was the next situation. Another reminder that, just like a movie, what matters now isn't as important as what happens next!

III.

PRODUCTION

Production - Physically being on-set to bring the prepared vision to life.

What if I told you that Filmmaking is an illusion? You are invited into the illusion, and I am the storyteller. I have one viewpoint, but another view reveals a different story.

Realize that there is no such thing as moving pictures. In a roll of film, there exists a collection of still images, but when they are passed through the gate of the projector, and when your eyes see this movement at a certain frame rate, your eyes perceive it as motion. It's an illusion of movement. This phenomenon is also referred to as the Persistence of Vision.

Filmmaking has a strange, yet fascinating history. This discovery is unconventional and often cited incorrectly by historians. Most people believe Thomas Edison created films, but he did not play a major role until he motioned to sue other inventors. Independent businessmen fled the states and relocated to Los Angeles to escape Edison's patents. Hollywood was born out of a desire to avoid Edison's intellectual property claims becoming the primary location for the film industry.

The original inventor of the film spectacle was a Frenchman by the name of Luis Le Prince. After his invention was internationally recognized, Thomas Edison motioned to sue claiming that he was the inventor.

In September of 1890, Le Prince boarded a train and was never seen again. Le Princes' Wife believed her husband's life was a murder plot orchestrated by Thomas Edison himself.

Here is another story about the discovery of motion pictures. A man named Leland Stanford, governor of California is at a horse racing event in Sacramento, CA. He strikes up a bet with another man, when horses gallop, all of their legs leave the ground. What makes this bet even stranger is that they hire the photographer

Edwaeard Muybridge to take multiple pictures to see if this is true. Muybridge places multiple cameras near each other, so when the horse passes, the photographs each snap a picture at the right moment. Leland wins the bet, all hooves leave the ground when a horse gallops.

Muybridge experiments with the pictures and puts them together. He realizes that when he does this, the pictures move. For the rest of his life, Muybridge dedicated himself to experimenting with motion pictures. He would bring various animals and people into a studio to record their movements. If you thought this story was strange, it gets even more interesting. Muybridge is also a murderer. He spends time away from his Wife to take pics. He kills his wife's lover after discovering the affair. The court gives Muybridge the death penalty, but he pleads insanity.

The idea of the film being seen as an illusion happened when a stage magician named Georges-Jean Méliès saw the Lumiere Brothers projecting their short film on a screen for an audience. The short film titled 'The Arrival of a

Train' [*L'arrivée d'un train en gare de La Ciotat*] depicted a steam engine train arriving at the station, however as the train approached the camera, audiences feared a real train would jump out of the screen. Méliès was fascinated that an invention that enamored a mass audience was merely an illusion. Once Méliès retrieved a portable camera, he went out to film on the streets. A piece of film broke, but it was this malfunction that inspired a new idea for his stage act. When the film was broken, the next piece could be edited to overlap the previous producing a 'jump in time.'

So, the illusion is that filmmaking is a series of still photographs, but when passed through a projector at a certain frame rate, they appear to move, much like a flip book. The modern frame rate of a movie is 24 fps. Why 24? Because anything passed this speed can make the audience sick. 24 fps allows the audience to keep up with the action and take in camera movements and most importantly, the story. And when filmmakers create an effect, they are using trick photography to manipulate the viewpoint. As filmmakers, we still enjoy tricking people to this day.

Production

Videography Jobs, Working with Clients & Conducting Business –

-       Types of jobs

-       Business (freelance vs. business)

Film/TV Production

In this video, I will discuss how you can work in the film/TV industry. I will discuss the mindset of working on-set and how to find jobs. [Below the Line & Above the Line Jobs]

-       Let's begin with Below-the-Line [BTL] PA jobs. You are on-set, not to get paid, you are learning what other positions might interest you.

-       Mindset & Method

-       Risk

- Work Hours

- Benefits

- Working w/ People

- Above-the-line [ATL] jobs & and being creative (mentality) (impulse)

Now that you know about Pre-production, here is a brief overview of Production.

Remember, Production is physically being on-set. Recording the camera, capturing the sound, and working with the cast and crew. All events in pre-production have led up to these moments.

In this lecture, we will identify the jobs in the film and video industry. There are thousands of jobs in the industry, so I will limit the discussion to the primary on-set positions. We will go over on-set jobs for filmmaking and videography.

Let's begin with filmmaking. There are 2 terms that you should familiarize yourself with – Above the Line and below the Line.

In a nutshell, Above the Line jobs are considered to be the creative workers driving the project.

Below the Line jobs are the employees executing the physical labor, building upon the creative decisions.

These terms exist based on old studio system regulations that determine the pay scale of workers attached to a movie.

Now that we understand the pay scale, below are some of the major positions on set.

ABOVE-THE-LINE

Director - Must exercise the skill of communication to fulfill the intended vision by translating the script to screen.

Screenwriter - The storyteller who brings the vision to life on the page as a blueprint for the director.

Producer - The creative/financial advisor executing the intended vision.

Actor - The character(s) being seen on-screen.

BELOW-THE-LINE

Assistant Director, [AD] – They work closely with the director and organize the production days. They command the set by problem-solving to mitigate risk. The Assistant Director overlooks the other departments and reports to the Director and other creatives about the overall approach to each shooting day.

Cinematographer – Is composing the lighting for the scene. They work closely with the Director to plan the shots for the movie. The cinematographer is not the camera operator but certainly can be.

Director of Photography [DOP] – Also synonymous with Cinematographer is the Director of the lighting department and holds the same position as Cinematographer, but with additional roles. The Director of Photography is more involved with each phase of production and can be on-site location scouting, assisting with color in the editing room, or being close to the camera department. They have more control over the image.

1st Assistant Camera [1st AC] - Assisting in the construction of the camera/equipment for the operator.

2nd Assistant Camera [2nd AC] - Also assisting, but manages the slate [clapperboard] so that the editor can sync the sound with the picture.

The Boom Operator [Boom Op.] – Holds the microphone intending to capture sound. They choose various microphones for specific set-ups.

Sound Mixer – Can also be the Boom Operator, and they work closely with the boom operator and use a device that preserves the captured sound.

The Camera Operator [Cam. Op]. – Operates the camera.

Character Generator(CG, or CGI) – A character entirely composed from a computer.

Digital Imaging Technician DIT – Transfers the data on set from the camera to storage devices.

Costume Designer – Designs the costumes for the actors

Composer – Creates the soundtrack

Dolly Grip – Organizes the dolly for moving set-ups

Editor – Takes out the bad bits and adds the good bits of footage for the screen

Gaffer – Managed under the lighting under DOF. The Gaffer physically sets up the lights on set.

Key Grip – Organizes and builds props

Line Producer – Makes sure the Production is staying within the budget.

Location Manager – Is searching for or locking locations for Production

Make-up Artist – Manages makeup for the actors

Production Assistant [PA] – This is the entry-level job on a set. Their jobs range from organizing the food, getting coffee, carrying equipment, watching equipment, completing office tasks, or directing crowds away from the set.

Script Supervisor – Manages the script on-set as well as looks for mistakes including continuity errors and changes on-set.

VFX– Creating visual effects

Foley– Re-creating sounds that were not captured on-set through the art and craft of re-recording.

Now let's look at the positions in **videography** –

The Client – Is hiring you to record a desired event. The client and videographer work together to create a contract that enables them to establish a business transaction.

The Videographer – Is recording the content and being paid for their efforts.

The Subject – Is the person of focus for the desired shoot.

The Green – Is getting paid that sweet money that you deserve. [*This bit is for laughs*]

Experience On-Set

You take away a new experience after working on every project. The experience, for better or worse, can push your career forward.

In the beginning, working on film sets can be daunting. On-set language is mostly contrived of slang. Understanding this language will assist in your education. [*See the common film set terms on pg. 73*].

I always encourage students to reflect on their set experiences instead of diving into working full-time. The student should focus on the job that interests them [if any]. The next bit of advice is based on experience.

Many young people work on film sets to satisfy their career ambitions, but what they lack is knowledge about the industry. I have met young people on sets who have dropped out of high school and college to pursue this industry full-time. This might have been an admirable endeavor for the industry of the past, but for the industry of today, I would advise against this idea. Young people should spend more time studying what interests them and forming relationships by networking with those knowledgeable about the subject matter. A young person who is not native to industry cities working full-time on sets must endure a fate where the majority of their time is spent traveling and not spending time with friends and family.

I have witnessed many who have embraced this way of living. They desire to work in this field to be something but consequently use work to escape mental struggles. I believe that working hard at something you do not know about to avoid something in your life is unwise and will most likely lead to misery.

I always hire people on set who are just as passionate about filmmaking as myself. We are in it for the creative process, not laboring over finances as a means to an end. Many of my friends work full-time in this craft and are happy to know their passions and interests have encouraged them to endure the jobs healthily.

I was on my first film set when I was eighteen years old. We were filming a movie trailer that was sure to be a hit, only to never get made!

Although I was upset about the film not being made, I befriended much of my crew and learned that being a film director was a difficult endeavor. As I grew older and wiser, I began working several positions on-set in major cities from Production Assistant to Gaffer to 1st Assistant Director.

Since I was familiar with the creative ends of the industry by working on my projects, I acquired enough experience to jump into the 1st Assistant Director role.

There is no working your way up in this industry. Recognize that your hard work on set means nothing, so long as you connect with others to communicate your career ambitions. The value you express in the department of your interest will provide opportunities for you to progress.

In the beginning, a young person most likely will work at an entry-level job as a Production Assistant [PA]. There are many roles that a PA satisfies on-set.

PA Roles On-Set

1. Office PA - Works in the office.

2. Runner - Travels to get food and/or craft services (crafty).

3. Lock-up - Loads/unloads equipment/watches equipment.

4. Set PA - Working on-set undergoing various jobs to assist with production.

5. Random Task PA [*This one is a joke, but most of the time it's true*]

Determine whether you would like to pursue the **creative** or **technical** ends of this industry. In my experience, the most desirable position to obtain is being a Set PA. As a Set PA, you are physically working in a production environment where other departments can see you, whereas in other positions (although important) it is difficult for others to see your work. A Set PA position can lead you to more opportunities, but most importantly this position allows you to see the on-set operations of other departments to determine where you might fit in.

I was provided more roles on-set after being a Set PA and found myself on both the technical and creative sides. I enjoy working on-set because every day is a learning experience and meeting like-minded people forms long-lasting friendships.

So, do your research. Determine what department interests you and go for it. The best jobs are when friends recommend you for set work, so be sure to choose your friends wisely.

Common Film Production Terms for the Set

Apple or **Apple Box** – a solid wooden box that comes in standardized sizes (from largest to smallest): full, half, quarter, pancake.

C47 – a clothespin

Crafty – craft services area and/or person

Day Player – a crew member hired for only one day or a handful of days' worth of work

Hot Points – yelled when carrying something with the potential to hit somebody like a dolly track or a C-stand. Usually said when going through a narrow hallway, doorway, or around a corner.

Last Looks – phrase to call in hair/make-up to give a final touch-up to actors before a scene is filmed

Magic Hour – the time right before sunrise/after sunset in which the sky is somewhat dark but still illuminated. Often lasts only 20 minutes despite its name

Martini – the last shot of the day

Picture's Up – phrase to alert all on set that cameras are almost set to start rolling

Sides – a half-sized script that contains only the scenes being shot that day

Sparks – an electrician; see "juicer"

Stinger – an extension cord

Talent – actor(s) or actress(es)

Video Village – the area in which viewing monitors are placed for the director and other production personnel.

Directing

Let us explore the role of the director, the mindset, and the lifestyle.

1. What is the Role of the Director?

2. What does it take to be a Director? Qualities?

3. How should one start becoming a Director?

4. What is the income of a Director?

5. How can I describe directing through experience?

The Director - Must exercise the skill of communication to fulfill the intended vision by translating the script to screen.

The Director is involved in the creative process, which includes overseeing every aspect of Production from start to finish. The Director's role is to translate the vision from the script to the screen and collaborate with the actors.

However, given the extensive role of the Director today, the director's inclusion in the process has changed.

Based on experience, I believe that not all people have the necessary attributes of a Director. It takes a leader (a specific type of mindset) to drive content. I think these attributes are based on personality and experience and how one carries themselves through hardships.

I believe that creative roles are the most labor-intensive jobs both physically and mentally. These are the most difficult jobs in the world. One moment you can have a deal with a studio, the next; things fall apart.

In my view, the most important lesson of being a director is learning how to work around rejection. You will have to learn how to pick yourself up, but if you find the positive in that rejection, it will enable you to change. Some people may associate rejection as a failure. However, if you learn from your mistakes, it is not failure, it is learning. The only person you are competing with in this industry is yourself. Your ideas will drive content, but if you do not have creative ideas, then this is not the role for you. One project can create success, but not a career. Only your ideas and intuition can do that.

Remember, filmmaking is 1% imagination, 99% perspiration. You have to try your best and understand how to carry your voice through the craft of storytelling.

I think problem-solving is the most essential aspect of directing because if something goes wrong, people look to you to fix it. Attitude is another quality of Production that impends the creative process. Ambition and perseverance will be the motivating factor to accomplishing the vision. Anxiety [for better or worse] will shape you. Expect to feel anxiety every time you walk on set. With practice, the anxiety will change over time.

If you want to become a Director, then you should be actively making movies. Those dreaming about it will not satisfy this role. This is a show don't tell industry. *It's Shut up and show me your work, or see you later, I'm not listening to a project that is not realized. I'm interested in the project you've done and what you are doing next!*

-       Make movies with your friends and family who want to grow with you, always.

-       You should be making short films to understand your style, vision, collaboration budgeting, and most importantly, learning about what it takes to make a movie.

-       After being comfortable with short films, it is best to enter film festivals (not to win) but to see how an audience reacts to your stories. Don't let the reward of winning get to your head. When you think you have performed well in a high-ranking festival, it is a good idea to think about where you want to go next.

-       Ask yourself: Is directing a career or a hobby? Do you want to make money, gain notoriety, or both? What are the next steps to achieving these goals?

-       If you are trying to do this as a potential career, then making a longer format film, Feature Film, could benefit you.

 I stress to students that an aspiring director should find their voice in their twenties and create a feature-length film in their late twenties/ early thirties. This advice is not to attack ageism, but the older you are the more complicated life can be.

In the beginning, I had goals for myself with short films – getting into prestigious festivals, winning, and selling short films. You should make goals for yourself too.

These choices were particularly hard for me to make when I was making short films years ago. I was extremely paranoid about negative reviews and audiences disliking my work, but after performing well in many festivals, I through those thoughts away, it wasn't until I sold all of my short films with the current extra stream of income, did I seriously considered taking my next steps.

If you choose the role of director, realize that you are choosing to be an entrepreneur. You are driving content and building an audience so you can make and sell films. If you do not understand business, finances, and scheduling, this is not the role for you.

As a filmmaker, you will struggle over financial stability and creative Freedom. Only some can balance both scales. You will have to be open to sacrificing your time hustling to make good content and constantly learn from your mistakes. You will have to change your way of thinking about the world, to achieve your goals.

A Director must have a vision for the story they wish to bring to life. The crew looks to the director after every take and you better have an answer. There is no time for 'I don't know.' You are going to know, or you are not going to be a sufficient director. **Know thy vision, by knowing thyself** – is the mantra.

-        If you are interested in becoming a Director for financial gain, walk away, you're not my friend. Directing is a part of the risk-taking industry. How much are you willing to lose? And if you answer that question, then you won't be a director. People become filmmakers for the pursuit of passion, not financial security.

-        Directing can be an overwhelming burden of regret, but I think seeing the end project is very rewarding, especially if you get your message and vision across. Unlike other arts, Directing is the most tedious and time-consuming, and your vision changes within that time. If you love movies, then I assure you, you can become a filmmaker.

Young aspiring director must open their minds to playing other roles much like a conductor of a symphony. A conductor does not have to know how to play every instrument, but they should know how each instrument sounds.

Go out and have fun, that's always an important element. Have fun and make films!

Producer - A person(s) who oversees aspects of Production by coordinating various aspects of film production, such as selecting the script coordinating writing, directing, editing, and arranging financing to a project's end.

A Producer is very knowledgeable about movies and the on-set operations. A Producer spends many years on a project, as they oversee each phase in production.

To summarize, there are many positions on a film set that you may want to familiarize yourself with to learn more about navigating the industry. You should also familiarize yourself with various roles in filmmaking/videography. Both mediums have similarities but range in price point and execution. Next, I discussed how to obtain jobs in the industry and place you into the mindset of the industry worker. If you are interested in a set position, do your research and go after it.

Let's look at the common ways to frame subjects utilized in both forms of media. Now that we are moving into camera composition, students should know the psychology of framing and how it affects the viewer.

Let's investigate the commonalities of these mediums through the use of framing.

Here are the 3 most basic shots in the video -

Wide-shot [WS] – Establishes the characters in the setting. The WS serves 2 functions – establishing the characters, and seeing the environment they are in. The WS is framed further away from the subject capturing their entire body in frame.

Medium Shot [MS] – Also called a mid-**shot** or waist **shot**, is a type of camera **shot in film** and television that shows an actor approximately from the waist up. A **medium shot** is used to emphasize both the actor and their surroundings by giving them an equal presence on screen

Close-up [CU] – In a CU we are closer to the characters and see their emotions with greater detail.

Every shot in the video is a variation based on these main shots. Each of them provides the psychology of distance and can exemplify the withholding, or revealing of information.

Now let's move on to framing your composition:

A Low Angle – This is when the camera is lower than the subject. This low Angle makes the subject appear larger in the frame to elicit power.

A High Angle - (AKA God's eye view, or bird's eye view) represents the vulnerability of the subject based on their small size in the frame.

The Point of View - Or POV, conveys what we are seeing from the subject's eyes. This situates the viewer into a subjective viewpoint as if experiencing an event ourselves.

Tilt/Oblique Angle – This is when the camera is slightly tilted to the side on the tripod. It emphasizes anxiety or impending doom.

Two Shot – This is an easy definition to remember, is two characters seen in a shot.

Over the Shoulder Shot (OTS) – Functions in 2 ways. The first is that the audience sees who a character is speaking to in the frame. 2nd, we see where the character is looking, and their eye-line maintains spatial relations with the other character.

Now that you know framing, it's up to you to choose which framing will fit the scene. There are no rules for ordering shots, and that's where the ability to choose can either help toward or against your intentions for telling the story. The strongest filmmakers understand the psychology of the framing and utilize it to help elevate the story.

My emphasis on the visuals is stressed because I feel like students feel that dialogue tells the story. The reason why this is untrue is because when you watch a video you are expected to see something visual first. We know this from silent films. Next time you watch a film or video, challenge yourself. Watch the video without sound. You will realize that the visuals, if effectively shot, tell the story.

Now then, can dialogue tell a story? Yes. This is called exposition in writing. A strong writer knows how to complement exposition through visuals. For example. Let us say there are too many characters in a room. One is trying to sell a watch to another – that's the exposition. But now I have to also convey this idea visually. So perhaps I have a shot where in the reflection of the glass, I see the emotion of the other person's face reacting to the exposition. Now it's more interesting because it's an intellectual way of saying, here is the importance of this dialogue visualized through framing.

So, remember, it's the visuals elevating the story. The dialogue only elevates visuals. If you compare a poorly shot film and a well-shot film, you will see the difference.

When I watch student films, this is a common mistake. Students think having good dialogue will make their story better. No, it's the visuals and the psychology, where the camera is faced, that will engage the audience emotionally.

Dialogue elevates the visuals always. And when we jump into acting, the same idea is true. When you understand visual literacy through practice, you will begin seeing its importance.

Another term of importance is Foreground & and background

Let's look at some examples and see how composition affects the viewer, and most importantly, tells the story.

Now let's look at Compositional Influencers. A compositional influencer is a guideline for our eyes to read an image.

Rule of Thirds – The most common areas of the screen where viewers look.

Golden Ratio – A pleasing guideline for our eyes that uses the shape of the setting to focus on the subjects.

Triangular Composition – Utilized to guide our eyes to 3 points in a frame.

Another example of triangular composition, but now it is in the form of art, Linear Perspective, conveys how our eyes are led to a 3D image. Renaissance artists used this technique in their paintings to give the illusion of dimension.

Now that we know the compositional influencers, let's see if you can spot them in the provided examples.

In summary, the Camera and composition help us identify the meaning of the visual elements presented on screen. Know these definitions well, to learn more about storytelling. Once you know these definitions and see their importance, we can move on to the technical elements of the camera.

Technicalities of the Camera

I'm interested in video, which equipment do you recommend I buy first? A question I hear every semester. It depends on your budget and your interests.

Before we begin. The common flaw I see with film students is that they believe owning expensive equipment will make their films better. This is untrue as it is the person operating the camera that is telling the story. Case in point, I shot 3 of my 4 short films that I sold [exhibition agreement] in 1080p HD with cameras that were 4 years old. Buying a bunch of equipment is not going to enhance your skill, but it sure burns holes in your pockets. It's all about not spending too much, or if you predict going into this long term, do tons of research before buying and this is where YouTube comes in. It's why I love

YouTube; I'm always learning about something! And there is a great videographer who does in-depth tests and review and showcase their equipment.

Investigate how to buy gear. I should mention that I prefer living a minimalist lifestyle and living frugally below my means. I am not interested in the new tech, new phones, or computers.

My total cost of film equipment (which is more of an estimation, because I am currently selling my old gear is close to $10,000 over the span of 10 years. That's not a lot of money. I buy only what I need. Usually, I can operate with using only one good lens, instead of purchasing many and having them rest in storage.

To review, compositional influencers are formulas for making images pleasing to the eye. They intend to draw the eye to certain areas of the frame, providing information that enables us to decipher the image to elicit an emotional response.

We've discussed the purpose of composition, so let's investigate how we can make sense of it.

In this shot, the triangular composition is used to convey seduction, and how one character overpowers the other by revelation of size comparison. In the background they are small, in the foreground, her leg is in the scene.

In this respect, the size of the subject in frame can help us realize whether a person is in control, or <u>change</u>. In this shot, there is space with plenty of headroom for the subject. It reads as an emotional moment, and the wind carries the sand away from the character. In some instances, filmmakers would cut to a close-up to convey the character's reaction, but in this shot, director George Miller acknowledges the empty desolate landscape, making the setting a character in itself.

Camera shots can also withhold information from the viewer like in the film 'The Fall.' In this shot, the costume design hides the face to create mystery.

Camera shots can also reveal information and the positioning of the subjects helps to identify character attributes. Balance and control are conveyed by the subject's positioning in the middle of the frame. In this shot, the subject is also addressing the viewer and because they are in the middle, we read the image as obtaining control, as they are the center of focus.

Unlike this image, there is a difference in headroom. Both images are wide shots, but the context is different. The camera is further away looking up as if the character is reaching out to find hope, while in this shot, the camera is centered on the character. Linear Perspective helps realize this emphasis of focus too. The filmmaker can control the audience's emotions by understanding how composition affects the viewer.

So, we understand balance & and how it relates to symmetry, but what about negative space? By providing emptiness, we know that the characters are distant, or lonely. In this framing, there is space in the middle, and there's headroom. This would be considered to be a mistake, as it is an asymmetrical image, but its intention exists to develop characters' thoughts or how they feel.

Since creators are making videos and films, understand they are making the rules for presenting the story, they are creating the language for the audience. Video is very much a universal language, but language can help situate the audience into the story. Filmmaking is all about choice. When you work in a studio, there are some limitations, so every choice you make matters. That's the difficult part about filmmaking. You have to make choices that can enhance or devalue the storytelling process. That is why this medium is difficult, with a handful of people trying to keep their careers consistent.

Now that you know the composition and interpreting the image, let's see how equipment can further enhance this notion.

Tripod – A 3-legged apparatus used to support the camera.

<u>Dolly</u> – A device utilized for directional camera movement.

<u>Steady-Cam</u> – A device used to stabilize the camera for moving shots.

<u>Handheld/Shoulder Rig</u> – An accessory used to balance the camera for a more stabilized shot.

~Camera equipment also includes lenses.

There are many lenses out there that each serves a desired purpose.

To summarize lenses – There are 2 different types. Primes & Telephoto. Each serves its purpose depending on your needs.

Lenses allow the filmmaker to control the image. Each glass has its aesthetic. You can desire a sharp image, an image with more contrast, a soft image, or an image with large or small bokeh.

The term bokeh is the size of the out-of-focus spirals in an image.

A lens can be spherical with spherical bokeh, or anamorphic, with cat-eye bokeh. It all depends on aesthetics and how you want the image to look for Production. I pay very close attention to lenses and always know the limitations and quality the image produces. I pay close attention to lenses because it is a part of bringing the vision to life.

I will overview the basic terms for lenses for this class.

Focus – controls the amount of detail that you want to convey in an image.

Focal Length – The overall space between the camera and the subject. There are a variety of different focal lengths. Here are the most common ones.

24mm – Is a Wide-angle perspective where subjects can be closer to or from the camera. A wide-angle lens distorts the sides of the image, stretching it.

50mm – The closest to how the human eye perceives an image (35-40).

85mm – Compresses the background, making it closer to the subject.

Here's how each focal length can be applied to further promote psychological awareness to the viewer. Let's look at the previous shots and I will determine the estimated focal lengths.

Filters – A piece of glass situated behind or in front of the lens that can create effects, or make the image appear darker. For example, I may use a Neutral Density [ND] filter for filming outside with harsh sunlight, so my image is not overexposed and retains detail. Or, I may use a filter for an effect for a film, and bring a hazy look to have light wrap around the subject's face.

Let's look at Prime Lenses – These lenses are smaller, lighter, and more compact and are known to let more light into the camera (depending on the camera, of course).

Prime lenses have a fixed focal length which means the focal distance cannot be manipulated. It always stays at one distance. Prime lenses are also known to be sharper than telephoto, as well as cheaper.

The Telephoto or Zoom lens has a variable focal length, which means you can change the focal distance depending on your needs. This is a convenience, but one with a cost. Telephoto lenses are more expensive than primes as they have many glass elements. Telephoto lenses may not let in as much light as primes, and they can be less sharp. They are also heavier in weight.

So there's a contrast between the lenses. OK, so which lens should you buy and which should you use on-set?

It depends on your preference and your path in videography. In my lens bag, I prefer prime lenses because they are smaller and are more desired for shooting movies. My lenses are not modern, they are vintage, which provides a specific aesthetic. Then I have 1 telephoto lens. It was more expensive, but I am able more versatility overshooting if needed.

Composing the shot also has a lot to do with the logistics of the shoot. For example, if I have a small budget, I may film hand-held or with a tripod. If I have access to smooth camera shots but want to move fast on-set, a Steadicam is more beneficial. It all depends on the productivity of the shoot. Again, choices that you will make.

In summary, understand how framing can elicit an emotional response from the audience. There are many tools that filmmakers have at their disposal from lenses to filters, it's not about the quality of the camera, it's about the quality of the operator. Know these terms to better familiarize yourself with the craft.

Students will most likely begin on Digital Single Reflex Lens or DSLR cameras.

The prices of DSLRs range from low to mid-budget. Larger cameras, video specific have a high budget. In RTV you can work with the Canon T6i's, the camcorders.

The Canon T6i shoots have both photo and video capabilities and can record in Full HD1080p.

The T6i is a touch screen and has a simple layout for all production needs. Above the camera is a dial that showcases the variety of options for shooting.

The only options you should know for this class are video mode and manual Mode 'M' as indicated on the dial.

The reason why we mostly use manual mode for video is for more control over the image.

For this class, if you own a DSLR, I highly suggest you learn the manual functions. Please do not rely on Automatic, because it is not reliable.

If you are using a phone, there are apps for manual mode, that I would recommend downloading for free, or you can use automatic mode if the before-mentioned options do not work. Bottom line – If planning to work in the video industry it's manual functions. There is even a role on set, 1st AD, who controls the focus on the camera, also called focus pulling.

I have only used manual functions. It may be challenging to comprehend at first, but practice will help you realize its importance.

Let's review the manual functions of the camera by understanding the 'exposure triangle.'

Shutter Speed - Adjusts the speed at which you capture/record the image. The higher the number on the shutter, the more time will appear frozen. The lower the shutter speed, will create a motion blur. Shutter speed is measured by fractional increments.

F-Stop - Serves two functions. The aperture lets in light and alters the depth of the field. The higher the number, the more detail is captured in your image. The lower the number, the less detail will be in your image rendering a shallow depth of field appearance. F-stop is measured by fractional increments.

ISO - International Standards Association concerns the light's sensitivity to the sensor of the digital camera. The higher the number, the more light enters the sensor. The lower the number, the less light enters. ISO is measured by hundreds.

LIGHTING

Lighting plays a functional role in the elements of storytelling. The cinematographer uses light as a tool for shaping, much like a painter uses a brush and colors to paint their canvas.

Story Time:

A man enters a dimly lit room. A mysterious figure comes out from the darkness. A light on the desk light reveals the mysterious figure to be a woman, now standing above the light. The man smiles, now recognizing her appearance.

Reflection:

The emanation of light is knowledge because we can see. If there is no light, if we have darkness, that information is lost meaning there is no image. Light is not created, it is shaped. Actors are positioned to unfold the story much like our example above.

Cinematographer - Their goal is not to create light, so much as to shape it. They take lighting that is already in a scene and manipulate the light to elicit mood. Lighting enhances the story.

In Old Hollywood, the intention of lighting a subject was to make them look beautiful, or masculine. In the industry of today, lighting is used intellectually as an aesthetic to satisfy the mood of the genre. Audiences today can see a style of lighting and associate that lighting with a genre. [Ex: A dark hallway elicits the genre of horror]. [Ex #2 - High key lighting with minimal shadows elicits the genre of romance].

The Cinematographer composes light for the film. The Cinematographer also makes creative decisions and is in charge of the lighting department. The Cinematographer works closely with the Director to create the overall vision. The other related title is Director of Photography who has more control over the image in all 3 Production phases.

Another worker in the lighting department is the Key Grip, who takes direction from the Cinematographer. The Key Grip relays the information to the Gaffers.

The Gaffers are physically placing the lighting and shaping the scene. They also have assistants called the 'Best Boy,' or 'Best Girl' who help shape the lighting for the set-up.

Essential tools used for shaping light that a Cinematographer may carry:

Flags, Scrims, Diffusors, Bounce boards.

Recognize that 2 sources of light exist in this world – Natural and Unnatural.

Natural Lighting comes from the sun or is the lighting that is already seen in the environment, already coming from a source? This lighting style evokes realism. You may see natural lighting in Drama, Thriller, and Action films.

Unnatural Lighting is artificially created to bring a certain effect to the scene. You may see unnatural lighting in Sci-fi, Fantasy, & Romance, or Comedy films representing a heightened sense of reality.

Both styles depend on your budget and the overall feel of the movie. For a low-budget film, natural lighting may be more desirable because it does not require many lights on set if not at all, giving flexibility to the shooting schedule.

Maybe a studio uses unnatural lighting, enabling them to control an interior scene. The budget might be higher or allocated to the lighting department, which can enhance the 'look' of the video.

There are 2 Types of Light Sources –

Hard Lighting – Creates sharp edges and shadows.

Soft Lighting – Wraps around the character and visibly softer on the skin.

The larger the light source, the softer the subject, as it can eliminate shadows. The further away the light, the more shadows are created.

But what about the sun? You may ask. The sun is a harsh source of light. But the sun is so far away, that clouds block it to soften light, or the sun sets, creating darkness. Only in daylight, do we see shadows from the sun. So anything blocking light can manipulate its shape. Go outside and put your hand up to see if there are any shadows, or what areas are changing the shape of the sunlight. Above all, observe light every day and see how it shapes your life.

Every cinematographer has their approach to on-set operations. As a cinematographer myself, I do not determine which lights should be in the scene. Instead, I use deductive reasoning to eliminate the possibility of how my lighting set-ups will affect the schedule. There is an old saying on-set - "Production is hurry up and wait." This quote applies to every department rushing to get ready for the day, but later having to wait for other departments to resume filming.

The two departments that will take up the most production time will most likely be lighting and make-up.

My approach to cinematography is minimalistic because my work as an Assistant Director has provided enough discipline to realize that time is money and in movies, there is never enough time and never enough money. <u>Simplicity is key.</u>

For an interior setting, I spend a lot of time observing the environment.

<u>Here are the questions that I ask myself on-set for an interior setting [in order]:</u>

1. Is this location interesting?

2. Can I use natural/ambient light?

3. What kind of practicals [prop light in the scene] can I use?

4. Are the plugs close to set, or are they far away?

5. Do I need to bring in a light? If so, how many?

I ask myself these questions by process of elimination. If I have to bring in light(s), the set-up time will be longer. Then there is a layer of safety that must be taken into consideration when rigging fixtures. I try my best to only use the practicals in the scene, or use one light source. You would be surprised about what you can execute by shaping only one light. While playing the role of Cinematographer, I shot my first feature-length film entirely with one light.

I think it is more necessary to bring in more lights when characters inhabit a room for a longer period. Otherwise, it's not worth the time and effort to set up a scene that the viewer will only see for a short amount of time.

A cinematographer must be economical. A common mistake that I see other cinematographers make on-set is their desire for a lot of equipment. I remember being on sets where we had entire grip trucks full of gear. Upon reflection, I realized all of this equipment is unnecessary and the budget could have been allocated elsewhere. You can do more with what is around you instead of relying on equipment to satisfy a particular look. You can achieve that same look with less.

For an exterior scene, I determine where the sunlight (if any) will be on the day/time of filming.

<u>Here are the questions that I ask myself on-set as a cinematographer for an exterior setting [in order]:</u>

1. What time of day will this scene take place?

2. Where is the sun?

3. How much time do we have to set up gear?

4. Where will the subjects be positioned?

5. Do I need to bring in a light, or gear? If so, how many?

I enjoy filming during magic hour [sunset/ sunrise], but also recognize that this is the most difficult time of day for filming because light and color are constantly changing.

The sun's direction determines the amount of time we have for the intended scene and also informs us about the temperature of the day.

I like to use natural lighting, but if we are bringing gear it is important to determine how much time everything will take. Then, based on the positioning of the subject, I can determine where the light will be.

As a cinematographer, your focus is to create a mood to convey the emotions of the scene. Recognize that I did not advise always relying on the emotions of the characters.

Here is an example:

In Krzysztof Kieślowski's *Three Colors: Blue* a woman sitting in a coffee shop is depressed about her husband's recent passing. Instead of conveying this emotion on her face, the cinematographer focuses more time on the woman observing a white sugar cube absorbing the coffee in her cup. This meditative visual idea is enough for the viewer to show not only how she feels, but also her recognition of change presented in the everyday. This is all remarkably explained in one camera shot, instead of modern American filmmaking which may rely on montage to over-emphasize an emotion.

Another example:

Director Paul Thomas Anderson holds close-up reaction shots of two lovers in the final act of *Phantom Thread* to convey how each character feels toward one another. The atmosphere is drowned in haze, creating an ominous ghostly effect, despite the genre being romance. Consequentially, the relationship is sustained by manipulation creating a haunting atmosphere and doubly resembles his deceased mother's presence in the place of his lover.

White Balance

As a camera operator, white balance determines the temperature of what you are capturing. White balance is measured by the Kelvin scale. Below is a helpful chart that will assist any filmmaker with associating the number with the time of day.

Degrees Kelvin	Type of Light Source	Indoor (3200k) Color Balance	Outdoor (5500k) Color Balance
1700-1800K	Match Flame		
1850-1930K	Candle Flame		
2000-3000K	Sun: At Sunrise or Sunset		
2500-2900K	Household Tungsten Bulbs		
3000K	Tungsten lamp 500W-1k		
3200-3500K	Quartz Lights		
3200-7500K	Fluorescent Lights		
3275K	Tungsten Lamp 2k		
3380K	Tungsten Lamp 5k, 10k		
5000-5400K	Sun: Direct at Noon		
5500-6500K	Daylight (Sun + Sky)		
5500-6500K	Sun: through clouds/haze		
6000-7500K	Sky: Overcast		
6500K	RGB Monitor (White Pt.)		
7000-8000K	Outdoor Shade Areas		
8000-10000K	Sky: Partly Cloudy		

Based on information from the book [digital] Lighting & Rendering
Chart and colors (c)2003 Jeremy Birn for www.3dRender.com

Audio

We are moving away from visuals and discussing audio. Did you know that audio commands 70% of a viewer's attention? You might be thinking, *'Mr. B you informed us that visual storytelling is the most powerful tool for this medium, so how can audio be more important than visuals?'*

Yes, I have conveyed how audio accompanies visuals, and that the story is dependent on the visual medium. But, audio invites us into that experience. Think about silent cinema. Musical scores were elevating the visuals. In this respect, understand that audio is utilized as an advantage to engage the viewer, emotionally.

An audience in a theatre is more likely to see a movie with poor visuals and excellent sound, rather than excellent visuals and poor sound. Why? Sounds that are not properly mixed are annoying and could damage one's hearing.

Next time you watch a video, try seeing how audio can enhance a scene. One of the most interesting elements about sound is that all sounds in a video and movie are essentially false. They are all manipulated to immerse the viewer in the experience. In this respect, audio has power, and understanding mixing will be an important tool for you to progress in video production.

The Boom Operator [Boom Op.] – Holds the microphone intending to capture sound. They choose various microphones for specific set-ups.

Sound Mixer – Can also be the Boom Operator, and they work closely with the boom operator and use a device that preserves the captured sound.

The **decibel** (abbreviated **dB**) is the unit used to measure the intensity of a sound. The decibel scale is a little odd because the human ear is incredibly sensitive. Your ears can hear everything from your fingertip brushing lightly over your skin to a loud jet engine.

Stand on a runway for an hour and you can lose your hearing. Be in a noise-proof room for an hour and you may go insane.

We are incredibly sensitive to sound and not only how we hear things, but when.

The loudness of sound is measured in decibels (dB). This is a measure of intensity, which relates to how much **energy** the pressure wave has. Decibels are a relative measurement. They relate the intensity of a pressure wave to normal pressure.

While many standard measuring devices, such as rulers, are *linear*, the decibel scale is *logarithmic*. This kind of scale better represents how changes in sound intensity feel to our ears.

Decibels are measured strangely. Anything above 0 is too loud. Anything below -84 is too quiet.

Usually, dialogue is edited at a decibel level of -12 to ---6db.

117

Soundtracks can either overpower dialogue or be less and ambient sound is usually set at -36db or below.

MUSIC & CINEMA

In an excerpt from the 1953 book *On Feeling & Form,* Susanne Langer defines art as the creation of forms symbolic of human feeling. *Expression* conveys a narrative that pertains to social conditions and exhibits signs of an effect, whether conscious or unconscious. These expressions are rooted in concepts and ideas. Music is symbolic of feeling because the medium depends on mood.

Human feeling is the starting point for art, but it is not an <u>expression of concept.</u>
Instead, music (in regards to the visual medium), is pattered sounds that recall analog emotional experiences. The listener retains this information through symbolic attributes of expression. Music has a dynamic structure of temporal influence, rendering the emotional experience. Music expresses feeling via an intimate historical influence that is created culturally [think Dies Eres] and the Gregorian chants from the Middle

Ages. The tonal influence of scales ascending or descending can induce power or doom. In filmmaking, music acts to punctuate emotional moments to further enhance the visuals presented on screen. Music also operates as an auditory recall for the character, setting, or story. Below are examples:

Jaws (1975)

Classical music operates through abstract symbols that carry the viewer through various states of mood by the method of the *leitmotif.*

Leitmotif - A theme throughout a musical or literary composition that re-occurs to intellectually remind the listener of an association with a particular person, idea, or situation.

A *leitmotif* might be audible for recall. For example, in the movie *Jaws* - the score by composer John Williams frequently uses the leitmotif to signal the approaching shark attack. Once the viewer hears the music, tension pulses through our veins. For Jaws music operates through psychological circumstances without the reliance on sight.

The Lord of the Rings: The Fellowship of the Ring(2001)

The music in The Lord of the Rings is cleverly orchestrated by the theme in the setting.

Musical Theme - A representation of a variation of music to elicit emotions.

Composer Howard Shore takes inspiration from Richard Wagner's 1857 opera: *The Ring Cycle [Der Ring des Nibelungen]* to highlight each of the settings that our characters traverse throughout the story. Each setting has a theme deeply rooted in the minds and hearts of the characters. The orchestral score swells with dynamic influence once the viewer recalls the theme. The theme also forwards character motivation. Instead of explaining the friendship of Sam and Frodo, it is expressed musically as one character encourages the other to leave their home and set off on a dangerous journey to destroy a powerful ring.

Star Wars I: The Phantom Menace

Every Star Wars film has a musical score for a specific character. Interestingly, fans of the franchise returned to the series to see how Anikan Skywalker became the evil Darth Vader, but many were left disappointed by not seeing Anikan's evolution in the movie. Director George Lucas avoided the quest for adventure outline from the previous trilogy and focused on the cause and effect of events and how a prophecy of a boy bringing balance to the force may alter political tensions in the galaxy.

The plot shifts gears to highlight the abilities of characters to showcase overcoming conflict to set up the effect of these relationships moving forward.

Character theme - Describes the inner thoughts, feelings, and desires.

Anikan's innocence as a boy alters his recognition of being freed from his homeland, only to be angered by the death of the person who believed in his freedom [Qui-Gon Jinn]. Anger stirs in Anikan, but this emotion is conveyed subtly through his reactions, but more effectively in his 'character theme' expressed as the credits end on Darth Vader's opening notes. The character theme in this instance changes from hope to anger which evolves in each episodic film moving forward.

IV.

POST-PRODUCTION

<u>Post-Production</u> - Taking what was captured in Production and re-constructing the footage for purposes of distribution.

<u>EDITING</u>

The editor's job is to take the footage captured in Production and polish the video product for viewing. According to Walter Murch, an Editor is someone who puts in the good bits and cuts out the bad bits.

The editor can work with the director to meet the needs of the intended vision. Editing is like completing a puzzle. There are so many pieces and once you put them together, the viewer sees the completed product. Did you know that people use to edit films by hand? Now, we use computers for editing purposes.

Non-linear editing is a non-destructive **editing** process. **Linear editing** was the method originally used with analog video tapes. ... **Non-linear** video **editing** is achieved by loading the video material into a computer from analog or digital tape.

Therefore, with computers, editors can edit out of order (nonlinear). There are a variety of jobs in the industry for editors. The primary jobs are – picture editor, sound editor, VFX-Additional Visuals through digital intermediates, SFX, and colorist.

The most fascinating aspect of editing is that this craft is motivated by feeling. There is no right way of putting together a video product. There is no mathematical or scientific explanation of why an edit should work. The entire medium is built upon human feeling.

There are hundreds and thousands of possibilities. In Walter Murch's Text, *In the Blink of An Eye*, he breaks down the mindset of the editor when completing a video project.

In Walter Murch's Book, he breaks down the 6 Criteria of editing, also referred to as the Rule of Six.

RULE NUMBER ONE: Emotion (51%)

Murch asks: *how do you want the audience to feel?*

Video functions by emotions with scientifically based answers. Everything you see is a function of feeling. I kept emphasizing the importance of visuals at the beginning of the semester because they elicit emotions through the medium of visual entertainment. Then, audio elevates the visual experience and together they evoke an emotional response for the audience.

Murch views Emotion as an invaluable resource. Without it, your movie is in trouble. The key point here: the audience should always be first in an editor's mind.

Murch is after a sort of expressionism when he explains that an emotional cut should take precedence over a cut that's only meant to preserve the continuity of the narrative. Emotion drives the story, not the story itself.

RULE NUMBER TWO: Story (23%)

Murch asks: *does the edit move the story forward in a meaningful way?*

This is essential. A story must be dynamic. There must be motion behind it; an underlying force hurdling the events forward. If the cut does not advance the narrative or make the audience feel they just put one foot forward, then that's trouble. Emotion and Story, Murch submits, are the most important. He leaves what tangibly moves a story forward up to the editor. All he asks is the editor's decision be "interesting" and "unique"

RULE NUMBER THREE: Rhythm (10%)

Murch asks: *is the cut at a point that makes rhythmic sense?*

One can assume that the reason why the last four rules are of less priority is not because they aren't important, but because they are implicitly (but vitally) linked to Emotion and Story. Murch likens them to "the bonds between the protons and neutrons in the nucleus of the atom." (20) He states that an editor should use an emotional cut if it serves the story AND the rhythm. If the rhythm is there, the audience will become unaware (or unconcerned) of lapses in continuity or the 180-degree rule.

RULE NUMBER FOUR: Eye Trace (7%)

Murch asks: *how does the cut affect the location and movement of the audience's focus in the frame?*

A cut must not disorient the viewer, to the extent that their eyes cannot comprehend the action. Action movies tend to be the main offenders of this rule, mainly because they must account for so much hyper-kinetic movement to keep up with the pace of the events.

RULE NUMBER FIVE: Two- Dimensional Plane of Screen (5%)

Murch asks: *is the axis followed properly?*

That said, a filmmaker/editor should learn the rules first before breaking them, or "crossing the line" [*See the 180-degree rule on pg.*

RULE NUMBER SIX: Three-Dimensional Space (4%)

Murch asks: *is the cut true to established physical and special relationships?*

Now that you know how to look for an edit, let's discuss the 2 different types of editing.

Realistic- Expands Time

Formal – Condenses Time

Next, let's define some important terms about editing.

A cut in editing is when a shot is an abrupt, but usually trivial film transition from one sequence to another. It is synonymous with the **term** edit, though "edit" can imply any number of transitions or effects.

Continuity – This is keeping within continuous action that directs the viewer's attention to a pre-existing consistency of story across both time and physical location.

There are several types of cuts in the video. I will present them here, but be sure to reference the video link for more information.

Now that you are familiar with the terms, this information will enhance your abilities for your next projects. I want you to edit your next projects using Murch's 6 Criteria for Editing.

Let's transition into various types of editing programs & and obtain a job as an editor. See what I did there?

Personal thoughts on editing – Everyone interested in videography and film should also know editing so you can make projects and build your portfolio. If you are interested in working as an editor, understand that it requires long hours being on-screen.

Now that we know something about editing, let's discuss the most basic form of structuring a scene by discussing Montage. There is an entire history of montage that can be discussed in a film class, so I will avoid the history and solely discuss the function. If you are interested in learning the history of Montage, check out Sergei Eisenstein, as he was known to experiment with the uses of montage.

A montage is categorized as a formal edit because it condenses time to tell a story. A montage is defined as a series of condensed shots edited together to describe an entire scene.
Here are the different types of montages that exist in media:
According to prominent Soviet director Sergei Eisenstein, there are five different types within Soviet Montage Theory: Metric, Rhythmic, Tonal, Over-tonal, and Intellectual.

Metric – A series of shots edited together with the pacing of the musical score.

Rhythmic – Metric Montage is used to establish a visual pace, then the Rhythmic Montage is used to keep to the pace, in both a visual and auditory sense.

Tonal – A series of shots used to convey thematic elements.

Overtonal – The Overtonal Montage is a sort of amalgamation of the four other types of montages: Intellectual, Metric, Rhythmic, and Tonal.

Intellectual - A series of shots edited to convey an intellectual effect. This can be symbolic, or meaningful to the character's affecting them emotionally.

Now that you know the types of montage, see how they can affect your video. Let's use the industry standard editing program Adobe Premiere.

COLOR GRADING IN ADOBE PREMIERE FULL TUTORIAL

Editing is a fascinating medium because it is motivated by feeling. There is no one right way to edit a video. There are thousands of possibilities. There are a variety of editors who edit sound, picture, and color.

Colorist - A colorist solely focuses on the color of the image.

I will discuss color theory for post-production, and then jump into my organized workflow. Every editor has their workflow, but it is always best to be organized. Okay, let's get started.

Now every camera, much like editing has its workflow as well. Study your camera well, to understand what you are capturing in your videos.
In Lumatree color, we can find images and color manipulation. According to Adobe Premiere, Lumetri means color.
Remember these terms, **Luminance** refers to brightness and **chrominance** refers to color. These terms will provide a basic understanding of the settings that you are manipulating.
Let's move on to discuss the scopes used by a colorist. These scopes provide a scientific explanation of the footage that you have captured. They are called Lumetri scopes because they provide a statistical measurement of color and exposure calculated by a computer.

In Production, we cannot always trust our monitors, but we can trust our scopes in Post because a computer provides more accurate information than a waveform monitor.

So let's define the basic terminology for color by looking at the tools found in Lumetri Scopes. If we access the Lumetri Scopes panel, we will see a variety of graphs that correspond to their waveform. A waveform corresponds to our video on the screen. A waveform measures the luminance of an image. Editors use this panel to correct for exposure as well as review the overall dynamic range within an image.

Let's talk about color correction. You can find this panel in the Basic Color Correction tabs. This is where we will correct, or enhance any technicalities within the image. So let's define this set of terms.

-Exposure controls the brightness or darkness of an image.

-Contrast - Manipulates the tonal range of the image

-Saturation defines the brilliance and intensity of a color(s).

-Highlights (Gain) are the brightest areas of an image.

-Shadows (Lift) are the tonal ranges of the midtones. The Midtones are in the middle of the waveform, also referred to as (Gamma)
-The Blacks control the darkest part of the image, located at the bottom of a waveform.
-White controls the brightest part of the image, on top of the waveform.
As an editor, correcting the color first is best before grading your image. Toggle the FX option here to see a before and after video. After correcting your image, make sure the White Balance is corrected. Then we can refine it with tint. To match with the next 'clip' we can go into 'comparison view.'
Let's move on to HLS Secondary. Hue, Saturation, and Luma (light), define the brilliance and intensity of a color(s). [Manipulate the Color wheel].
If we want to pinpoint a specific area, we can add a mask to the image and manipulate that specific section. We can also track a subject's movement by activating the track forward button. Now that we have finished Color Correcting, let's move on to grading.

Color grading is processing a look for your video. This look can be applied with a LUT AKA look-up table that will provide a layered appearance for your video based on the camera's profile. You can find different profiles in most modern cameras. Some of the consumer DSLRs do not have these functions, but you can always change your camera settings to Neutral Tones, or try reducing colors.

Remember, always complete your color correction first, before finalizing a grade. This will reduce editing time and grading accuracy. Grading will be your final step before picture lock.

The primary terms concerning color are Hue, Saturation, and Luma.

-Hue is colors

-Saturation is the vividness or intensity of colors

-Luma is brightness or shade of hue

-RBG, or red, blue, and green – are the primary colors of light described in a waveform, but separate the luminance values in individual channels for a more accurate reading. With the RBG parade, the editor sees where these colors rest on a scale. It measures saturation from these channels. RBG Parade helps balance the image for the editor. For a well-balanced image, each of the 3 colors should roughly be equal.

A vector scope measures the chrominance (color components) of a video signal, including hue and saturation.

-The Vector scope is also related to saturation, but specifically pinpoints which colors are over and under-saturated. Colors reaching the outer areas represent saturation and whether they are inside or outside of broadcast limits. 75% saturation represents the maximum saturation for broadcast, so these areas provide awareness of where the intensity of color will spill. Aligning this line toward the middle of the vector scope conveys accuracy in skin tones.

Here are other Vector scopes – YUV – Luma / Croma concerns how much of a certain color is in a shot. The YUV Vector scope uses the more familiar YUV color space including color targets to display the pixel distribution in your images more intuitively.

Vector scope HLS – Hue, Luma (light), and Saturation defines the brilliance and intensity of a **color**(s).

Let's move into my workflow for coloring and grading.
-Adjustment Layer

In conclusion, Cinema is a beautiful art form because its language is universal and the ideas behind images are motivated by feeling. Every facet of artistic labor must be emphasized to universally construct a singular vision.

Cinema is access to a new perspective that can become a source of enlightenment because it is a relatable, shared experience.

CONCLUSION

Recognize that the visual medium is a 'show' don't tell' industry. Talking only gets you so far, but if you're not showing what you're made of, nobody will invest in you. This is one of the largest problems with the industry today - Too many fake content creators -You see tons of advertisers, gurus, and YouTubers trying to sell you content to provide their experience, but they have nothing to show. Why? Because they are too busy talking and making videos for YouTube instead of making movies. You can always lose money, relationships, or material items. In any case, you can gain all of these materials back because they are not a 'necessity,' they are 'commodities.'

Always try something, instead of nothing. It's hard to get anywhere when you are afraid of something that may not even exist. Hang around people who try to get better, or are already there. They will teach you more about life than the losers trying to convince you that they've faired better by being comfortable. Hang around with losers and be a loser. You cannot change a loser, but you can change yourself. Change yourself and watch your fortune change.

If you have gotten this far in the text, the next bit of information comes from the teachings of the Ancient Stoics, which may serve as a guide for your journey in pursuing film production.

In a world where social media platforms encourage us to share every moment of our lives by documentation of thoughts, it may seem counterintuitive to keep things to ourselves. The more we talk about our plans, the more we deviate from our focus by prematurely giving away our goal when it is in its infancy. The most uninteresting people that I have encountered are the ones who have informed me what they do, yet have little to nothing to show for this to be evident.

Our fulfillment should not depend on external validation. True contentment exists from within.

Think of your dreams like you would a plant.

When you begin your path in any pursuit, you begin as a delicate sapling that has just sprouted. If you pre-maturly share your dreams with others their doubts or criticisms may become like harsh winds that threaten to uproot your sapling. Recognize that people are also like plants. They can stunt your growth, or help you grow. One should instead nurture their dreams in order to strengthen their roots.

Now imagine harnessing the wisdom of obscurity knowing that the pursuit of recognition and fame is fleeting, hollow, and altogether harmful. In the privacy of your own thoughts and actions, you can gain strength in yourself, as the opinions of others should not impede your aspirations. The joy of authenticity in your own journey matters. Many are led to believe that your life depends on your happiness. This is untrue because happiness is fleeting. If I learned anything from filmmaking it is that authenticity is a prized *virtue* in today's world. Virtue outweighs happiness because it produces an ever-growing vine of purpose. The virtue that everyone has innate in them is to be a part of another's story.

Observe and focus on the world through the lens of empathy. Begin your story there.

"A short pencil is usually better than a long memory any day."
- Fortune Cookie

*

Life does not provide answers, it only makes us question.

What is my place in the world? A question that can be revealed through experience. Is this experience our own, or through the eyes of another? What does it mean to be human? Everything we see is perspective.

We exist in this world to move forward with understanding the meaning of our existence. Part of learning more about our interests is being curious.

In the world of cinema, we take a step outside of our perspective to take an observable approach to study others, and to find our place in the world. To discover what we find is useful for our lives can educate the minds of others.

Every question that you have about justice, happiness, good, evil, God, and existence are all theories about the nature of reality. Some people believe that philosophy is made to destroy your basis of believing in reality, but studying the academic principles of philosophy embraces the truth about reality.

Reflection on The Kybalion

***The Kybalion: (A Study of the Hermetic Philosophy of Ancient Egypt and Greece*)** is a book originally published in 1908 by "Three Initiates" about the teachings of Hermes Trismegistus.

It shares with ancient and medieval Hermetic texts several traits such as philosophical mentalism and spiritual enlightenment. The Kybalion is a critical tool for the transmutation of the physical and spiritual planes of existence.

In the ancient world, the lessons contained in this book have been maintained with secrecy. The reason for this concealment is due to the persecution of their followers.

This text is significant because it reveals the universal truths of our world in the form of principles.

When you learn to apply universal laws, you will possess the key to performing mental transmutation, empowering the individual to adjust to the vibrational states of nature. You have the power to change your reality with your mind.

The ancient sage Hermes Trismegistus is the spiritual source of the Kybalion. His teaching of the hermetic laws dates from over 5,000 years ago. The Egyptians attribute him to the god: Thoth. The Greeks – Hermes and Romans: Mercury.

His wisdom reached many continents. He created the concept of astrology, which later became astronomy. The purpose of writing this text was to show people that harmony exists in the universe by understanding the universal laws, so one can control what they manifest in their life.

The tangibility of reality is merely tricking our consciousness into thinking our world is as we perceive it when it is our interpretation of the information and whatever we manifest may only be a dream.

But this book sets out to show the reader that our lives are the only reality that we know, providing us with a meaningful existence. One of the thematic aspects of the Kybalion is Mentalism. This is conveyed through alchemy. This principle explains the nature of power and energy of the mind.

"The alchemists use this knowledge to connect with the innermost self and through connection, bring balance into one's life." – The Kybalion

One of the primary concepts of the Kybalion is that we live in a mental universe. All is mind. Everything is interpretation. However, understanding how to obtain an acute awareness of vibrational synchronicity will enhance intelligence. This is the key to taking control of your life and living as you truly desire.

Hermes Trismegistus (Egyptian transcription: The great of the great) may be a human or a god. Hermes in Ancient Greek is the god of wisdom. In Ancient Egypt, Hermes and the Nephanites, (wise men), traveled to the four corners of the world to obtain knowledge. Together they documented their experiences to define universal truths.

The book consists of wisdom about reading the hidden symbols in the world and how to further understand our universe.

This text will help one recognize the importance of philosophy.

Below are the core laws in *The Kybalion*.

The first philosophical idea arises from mental transmutation, the beginning of philosophy.

- The lips of wisdom are closed, except to the ears of understanding.

- Where fall the footsteps of the Master, the ears of those ready for his Teachings open wide.

- When the ears of the student are ready to hear, them cometh the lips to fill them with Wisdom.

- The Principles of Truth are Seven; he who knows these, understandingly, possesses the Magic Key before whose touch all the Doors of the Temple fly open.

The central concept in this book surrounds the 7 hermetic principles:

1. The principle of mentalism

"The All is Mind; the Universe is Mental."

2. The principle of correspondence

"As above, so below; as below, so above." This principle embodies the truth that there is always a correspondence between the laws and phenomena of the various planes of being and life represented through the symbols in nature.

3. The principle of vibration

"Nothing rests; everything moves; everything vibrates." The world is always moving even if we cannot visibly see movement from our perspective.

4. The principle of polarity

"Everything is dual; everything has poles; everything has its pair of opposites; like and unlike are the same; opposites are identical in nature but different in degree; extremes meet; all truths are but half-truths; all paradoxes may be reconciled."

5. The principle of rhythm

"Everything flows, out and in; everything has its tides; all things rise and fall; the pendulum swing manifests in everything; the measure of the swing to the right is the measure of the swing to the left; rhythm compensates."

6. The principle of cause and effect

"Every cause has its effect; every effect has its cause; everything happens according to law; chance is but a name for law not recognized; there are many planes of causation, but nothing escapes the law."

7. The principle of gender

"Gender is in everything; everything has its masculine and feminine principles; gender manifests on all planes of existence.

Frequently Asked Questions by Students

When I make films, do I have to hire a crew for all jobs on-set?

No, this decision is entirely reliant on you and the budget. Independent films do not have the flexibility of budget. Studio films do, so you are more likely to see a larger crew attached to studio films.

Do I have to go to film school to get these jobs, or have a career in the industry?

It's controversial, but the short answer is no.

An aspiring filmmaker must weigh their options to a financial end. In my early years, the question I asked myself was - Am I willing to lose $100k+ by going to film school to learn how to use a camera, or possibly be 100k+ in debt making my own films?

I chose to make films and not attend film school. The best part is that I have incurred no debt!

Overall, an academic education does yield significant benefits. You can meet like-minded people and possibly form life-long relationships. You are also capable of learning the medium faster than discovering it on your own. I knew I would struggle with this and made it a point to teach myself every position on-set, then make my connections. The process would take longer, rendering a slower learning curve over an accelerated one.

What equipment should I purchase?

A camera and a computer with an editing program is the most essential tool that can provide job opportunities. Do not work and live beyond your means.

How does one work in the creative roles?

The career you seek is the one you make. Let your journey inspire you. Curiosity is a window into existence.

Most student filmmakers focus on the creative ends and do not understand the business side of the industry. In this respect, I think young filmmakers today should be proficient in all creative positions and work within their financial means.

Why don't you give young filmmakers advice about the film industry?

My only advice to any aspiring or emerging filmmakers is to make movies. Oftentimes I am asked to critique student films of young directors, but I do not think my opinion matters. I share the same advice that another industry relative gave me when I chose to direct as a career choice. They said, "I guess you will have to make films." For years I felt that this advice was vague, but over time I've recognized that it is truthful.

A young film director's experience is their journey. I cannot change what a young filmmaker thinks they know. This can only be experienced through self-discovery. My role as a professor is to encourage students to reflect on their work to learn. In regards to projects, I always tell students "The edit is the truth. Everything in the edit should inform you about how to progress." When a student identifies the issues of their edit, they are learning about how to improve upon their skills instead of relying on my critiques. This is called learn by doing and it has served me well since birth!

"When the student is ready the teacher will appear. When the student is truly ready, the teacher will disappear."

- A Wise Sage

GLOSSARY OF POSITIONS ON-SET

There are thousands of roles in a movie, but this is a condensed list of the main roles for a budget of $0-500k production.

Director

Producer

Writer

Cinematographer

Actor

Boom Op. / Mixer

1st AD

Cam. Op.

1st AC

2nd AC

Line Producer

PA

Editor

Foley Artist

Make-up

Script Supervisor

VFX

Colorist

ABOUT THE AUTHOR

If you enjoyed reading this book, or want to learn more follow me on Instagram here - https://www.instagram.com/paul_bestolarides/

Feel free to 'like' and 'subscribe' to my YouTube channel to see more behind the scenes here - https://www.youtube.com/channel/UCewDtgIJY3Pno4VBKgIK_bw

If you are interested in reaching out you may send an e-mail to this address - pbesto@hotmail.com

UPDATES TO VERSION II

THE SECOND EDITION OF THIS TEXT WILL INCLUDE QR CODES FOR ACCESSING PICTURES AND VIDEO CONTENT.

YOU MAY REACH OUT TO SUGGEST REVISIONS FOR THE NEXT UPDATE.